DEDICATION

Also by Keith W. Jennison

VERMONT IS WHERE YOU FIND IT

THE MAINE IDEA

DEDICATION

TEXT AND PICTURES OF THE UNITED NATIONS

Arranged by

KEITH W. JENNISON

NEW YORK: HENRY HOLT AND COMPANY

DEDICATION

THE words of this book are selected from speeches by leaders of the United Nations. They come, as the pictures do, from many sources. Together they make one voice— the voice of the free people of the world.

K. W. J.

WHETHER we like it or not . . .

whether we realize it or not . . .

the fact is that history has launched this
generation into a revolutionary epoch.

The world which we knew in 1939 is a world which, for all practical purposes, belongs to antiquity.

Those of us who may be reluctant to accept the passing of the old order—who were fortunate enough to enjoy such security and privilege as it bestowed—

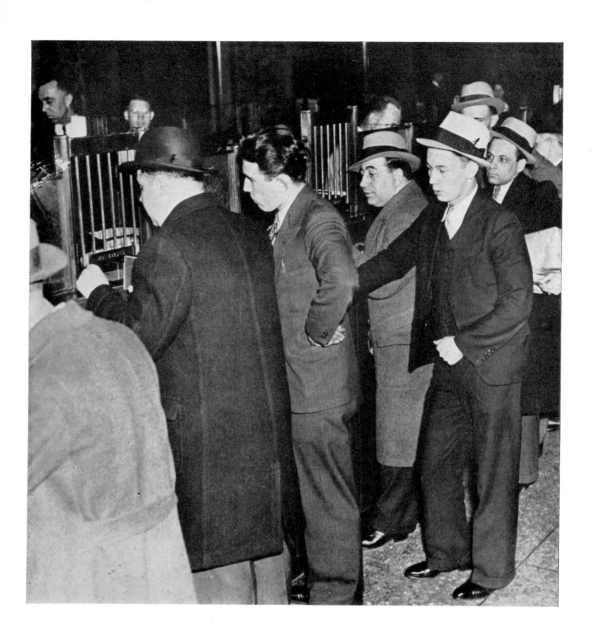

must remember that it was the order in

which Hitler was bred . . .

in which he found a ready audience for the evil doctrines that have now brought anarchy without precedence.

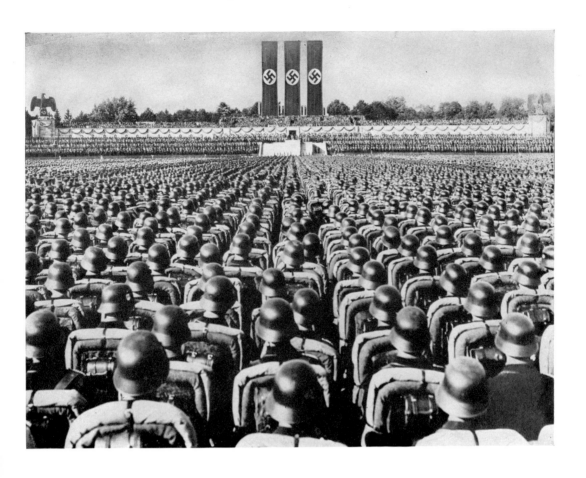

We are now in the midst of a war,

not for conquest,

not for vengeance,

but for a world in which this nation, and

all that this nation represents, will be safe

for our children.

In this war of liberation we shall not be alone.

For us no comfort can equal that of the certitude of fighting for an ideal shared by millions of men who refuse to accept slavery for themselves or impose it on others.

The aim we and our allies have set before us in the present war is freedom and security for humanity and its civilization.

We have planned our transport to crush the militarist criminals of Berlin and Tokyo and Rome.

We have pooled the shipping tonnage of

a dozen nations;

we have shared our foodstuffs,

our minerals,

our raw materials and our oil;

we have harnessed the constructive genius
of mankind to the furtherance of a single
cause.

You ask what is our aim? It is victory—

victory at all costs,

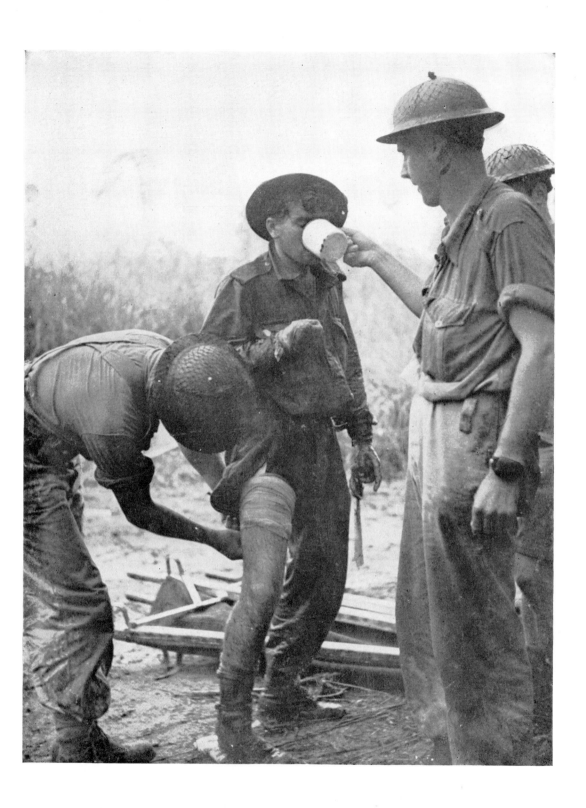

victory in spite of all terror,

victory however long and hard the road may be; for without victory there is no survival.

We shall fight on the beaches,

we shall fight on the landing grounds,

we shall fight in the fields and in the streets,

we shall fight in the hills;

we shall never surrender.

The United Nations are going to win this
war.

But it is useless to win battles if the cause
for which we fought these battles is lost.

We will not sever the bonds forged in the common danger. We will remain political and economic allies of those on whose side we fought.

We will dress the wounds of our people.

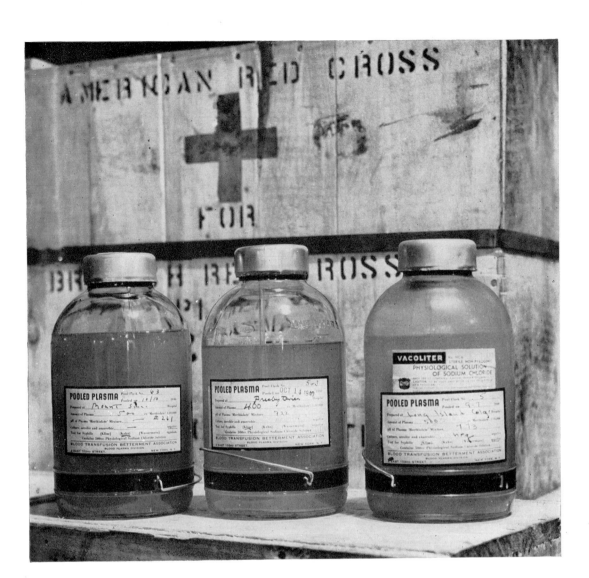

We will not forget those who bore the burdens,

battles

and persecutions.

We must look to the future, not to the past. Out of the ruins of the old we must build new institutions for the service of humanity.

We must solemnly resolve that in our future order we will not tolerate the economic evils which breed poverty and war.

The march of freedom of the past one hundred and fifty years has been a long-drawn-out people's revolution. The people's revolution aims at peace and not at violence; the people are on the march toward even fuller freedom than even the most fortunate have hitherto enjoyed:

The right of men, rich and poor, to be
treated as men;

the right of men to make the laws by
which they shall be governed;

the right of men to work where they will

at what they will;

the right of womankind to the serenity
and sanctity of the home;

the right of old men and women to the

tranquillity of their sunset;

the right to speak the truth in our hearts;

the right to worship in our own way, the
God in whom we believe.

The determination of free men and women everywhere must now be exercised to the full limit of endurance.

It is rather for us to be here dedicated to the great task remaining before us—that from these honored dead we take increased devotion to that cause for which they gave the last full measure of devotion—that we here highly resolve that these dead shall not have died in vain.

ACKNOWLEDGMENTS

PAGES	SPOKESMAN	PICTURE	CREDIT
2, 3	Walter Nash, Minister to the United States from New Zealand Sept. 23, 1942	Americans register for sugar rations	Charles Phelps Cushing
4, 5	"	Crowd around war bulletin in Times Square, New York City	Charles Phelps Cushing
6, 7	"	Bolt of lightning	Charles Phelps Cushing
8, 9	"	The great wall of China, third century B.C.	Keystone View Company
10, 11	"	Bank interior	Press Association, Inc.
12, 13	"	A Hitler speech	European
14, 15	"	National Socialism in the Luitpold Arena	British Combine
16, 17	Franklin D. Roosevelt Dec. 9, 1941	Waterloo Station, London	British Combine
18, 19	"	American troops arriving in Ireland	U. S. Army Signal Corps photo from European
20, 21	"	Italian prisoners	British Combine
22, 23	"	Belgian refugees	United Nations Information Office
24, 25	Joseph Stalin July 3, 1941	American troops and British Commandos	British Press Service
26, 27	General Charles de Gaulle Jan. 9, 1941	Chinese soldiers at the Yellow River Front	Clare Boothe from European
28, 29	Generalissimo Chiang Kai-shek Oct. 10, 1942	Hardanger Fjord, Norway	James Sawders from Cushing
30, 31	P. J. Noel Baker, Parliamentary Secretary to the Ministry of War Transport, Great Britain May 7, 1942	British tanks	British Combine
32, 33	"	Convoy in South Pacific	U. S. Navy photo
34, 35	"	New Zealand wheatfield	James Sawders from Cushing
36, 37	"	Open hearth furnace, Magnitogorsk	Sovfoto

PAGES	SPOKESMAN	PICTURE	CREDIT
38, 39	"	Texas oil well	Charles Phelps Cushing
40, 41	"	Birmingham blast furnace	Charles Phelps Cushing
42, 43	Winston Churchill May 13, 1940	Wounded Australian on the New Guinea Front	International News Photos
44, 45	"	The bombing of Singapore	Wide World Photos
46, 47	"	Nazi Infantrymen	Press Association, Inc.
48, 49	Winston Churchill June 4, 1940	Allied Troops in the North African invasion	British Combine
50, 51	"	American Paratroops	Press Association, Inc.
52, 53	Winston Churchill June 4, 1940	Men of a worker's battalion in the defense of Stalingrad	Sovfoto
54, 55	"	Japanese coastline and hills	Press Association, Inc.
56, 57	"	British mine-sweeper	British Combine
58, 59	Franklin D. Roosevelt August 21, 1942	Armada	Wide World Photos
60, 61	Franklin D. Roosevelt October 12, 1942	Guadalcanal	Press Association, Inc.
62, 63	Pieter S. Gerbrandy, Prime Minister, Netherlands January 13, 1941	On the march toward Syria	United Nations Information Office
64, 65	"	Pooled plasma	British Combine
66, 67	"	Polish refugees	United Nations Information Office
68, 69	"	Lybian warfare	European
70, 71	"	Internment camp in France	Wide World Photos
72, 73	Walter Nash July 11, 1942	Paris under bombardment	United Nations Information Office
74, 75	Herbert V. Evatt, Attorney General, Australia October 1, 1942	Unemployment, New York City	Erik Styrlander from R. I. Nesmith
76, 77	Henry A. Wallace, Vice-President of the United States May 8, 1942	New England	George French from R. I. Nesmith

PAGES	SPOKESMAN	PICTURE	CREDIT
78, 79	W. L. Mackenzie King, Prime Minister of Canada Sept. 1, 1940	Russian farmers with neck tags which the Germans forced them to wear	Sovfoto
80, 81	"	Senate Chamber of the Canadian Parliament	Press Association
82, 83	"	Shepherd in upper Alsace	James Sawders from Cushing
84, 85	"	A young Russian mother fleeing from the Nazis	Sovfoto
86, 87	"	Country home	Richard Hoit from Cushing
88, 89	"	A Lieutenant of a Royal Navy Fighter Squadron after escaping from the Germans	British Combine
90, 91	"	A young refugee from Luxembourg	United Nations Information Office
92, 93	Sumner Welles, Under Secretary of State July 22, 1941	Defense workers	Charles Phelps Cushing
94, 95	Abraham Lincoln Nov. 19, 1863	New England Church	Charles Phelps Cushing